interchange

FIFTH EDITION

3A

Workbook

Jack C. Richards

with Jonathan Hull and Susan Proctor

CAMBRIDGE UNIVERSITY PRESS

CAMBRIDGE
UNIVERSITY PRESS

University Printing House, Cambridge CB2 8BS, United Kingdom

One Liberty Plaza, 20th Floor, New York, NY 10006, USA

477 Williamstown Road, Port Melbourne, VIC 3207, Australia

314–321, 3rd Floor, Plot 3, Splendor Forum, Jasola District Centre, New Delhi – 110025, India

103 Penang Road, #05-06/07, Visioncrest Commercial, Singapore 238467

Cambridge University Press is part of the University of Cambridge.

It furthers the University's mission by disseminating knowledge in the pursuit of education, learning and research at the highest international levels of excellence.

www.cambridge.org
Information on this title: www.cambridge.org/9781316622773

© Cambridge University Press 1995, 2017

This publication is in copyright. Subject to statutory exception
and to the provisions of relevant collective licensing agreements,
no reproduction of any part may take place without the written
permission of Cambridge University Press.

First published 1991
Second edition 1998
Third edition 2005
Fourth edition 2013
Fifth edition 2017
Fifth edition update published 2021

20 19 18 17 16 15 14 13 12 11 10 9 8 7 6 5 4 3

Printed in Great Britain by CPI Group (UK) Ltd, Croydon CR0 4YY

A catalogue record for this publication is available from the British Library.

ISBN 978-1-009-04052-5 Student's Book 3 with eBook
ISBN 978-1-009-04053-2 Student's Book 3A with eBook
ISBN 978-1-009-04054-9 Student's Book 3B with eBook
ISBN 978-1-009-04075-4 Student's Book 3 with Digital Pack
ISBN 978-1-009-04077-8 Student's Book 3A with Digital Pack
ISBN 978-1-009-04078-5 Student's Book 3B with Digital Pack
ISBN 978-1-316-62276-6 Workbook 3
ISBN 978-1-316-62277-3 Workbook 3A
ISBN 978-1-316-62279-7 Workbook 3B
ISBN 978-1-108-40711-3 Teacher's Edition 3
ISBN 978-1-316-62230-8 Class Audio 3
ISBN 978-1-009-04079-2 Full Contact 3 with Digital Pack
ISBN 978-1-009-04080-8 Full Contact 3A with Digital Pack
ISBN 978-1-009-04081-5 Full Contact 3B with Digital Pack
ISBN 978-1-108-40307-8 Presentation Plus 3

Additional resources for this publication at cambridgeone.org

Cambridge University Press has no responsibility for the persistence or accuracy of URLs for external or third-party internet websites referred to in this publication, and does not guarantee that any content on such websites is, or will remain, accurate or appropriate. Information regarding prices, travel timetables, and other factual information given in this work is correct at the time of first printing but Cambridge University Press does not guarantee the accuracy of such information thereafter.

Contents

Credits

The authors and publishers acknowledge the following sources of copyright material and are grateful for the permissions granted. While every effort has been made, it has not always been possible to identify the sources of all the material used, or to trace all copyright holders. If any omissions are brought to our notice, we will be happy to include the appropriate acknowledgements on reprinting and in the next update to the digital edition, as applicable.

Key: BL = Below Left, BR = Below Right, C = Centre, CL = Centre Left, CR = Centre Right, TC = Top Centre, TL = Top Left, TR = Top Right.

Illustrations

337 Jon (KJA Artists): 51; **Mark Duffin**: 31, 80; **Pablo Gallego** (Beehive Illustration): 10, 20; **Thomas Girard** (Good Illustration): 4, 28, 53; **Dusan Lakicevic** (Beehive Illustration): 1, 14, 22, 33, 96; **Yishan Li** (Advocate Art): 6, 13, 65; **Quino Marin** (The Organisation): 29; **Gavin Reece** (New Division): 3, 64; **Paul Williams** (Sylvie Poggio Artists): 15, 66.

Photos

Back cover (woman with whiteboard): Jenny Acheson/Stockbyte/GettyImages; Back cover (whiteboard): Nemida/GettyImages; Back cover (man using phone): Betsie Van Der Meer/Taxi/GettyImages; Back cover (woman smiling): PeopleImages.com/DigitalVision/GettyImages; Back cover (name tag): Tetra Images/GettyImages; Back cover (handshake): David Lees/Taxi/GettyImages; p. 2: Michael H/DigitalVision/GettyImages; p. 5 (TL): Jade/Blend Images/Getty Images Plus/GettyImages; p. 5 (TR): Jamie Grill/GettyImages; p. 5 (BL): Blend Images - Jose Luis Pelaez Inc/Brand X Pictures/GettyImages; p. 5 (BR): Tomasz Trojanowski/Hemera/Getty Images Plus/GettyImages; p. 7: John Rowley/Photodisc/GettyImages; p. 8: KidStock/Blend Images/GettyImages; p. 9: monkeybusinessimages/iStock/Getty Images Plus/GettyImages; p. 12 (TL): ColorBlind/The Image Bank/GettyImages; p. 12 (TR): Sigrid Gombert/MITO images/GettyImages; p. 12 (CL): 4x6/E+/GettyImages; p. 12 (CR): Roy Hsu/Photographer's Choice RF/GettyImages; p. 13 (TR): mediaphotos/iStock/Getty Images Plus/GettyImages; p. 16: Purestock/GettyImages; p. 17 : PeopleImages/DigitalVision/GettyImages; p. 18: Phil Boorman/Cultura/GettyImages; p. 19 (TL): Robert George Young/Photographer's Choice/GettyImages; p. 19 (BR): dangdumrong/iStock/Getty Images Plus/GettyImages; p. 21 (TR): Chris Dyball/Innerlight/The Image Bank/GettyImages; p. 21 (CL): MattStansfield/iStock/Getty Images Plus/GettyImages; p. 23: EXTREME-PHOTOGRAPHER/E+/GettyImages; p. 24 (Johnson): George Doyle/Stockbyte/GettyImages; p. 24 (Marshall): Digital Vision./Photodisc/GettyImages; p. 24 (James): Yellow Dog Productions/The Image Bank/GettyImages; p. 24 (Grant): wdstock/iStock/Getty Images Plus/GettyImages; p. 24 (Simpson): Dave and Les Jacobs/Blend Images/GettyImages; p. 25 (TR): asiseeit/iStock/Getty Images Plus/GettyImages; p. 25 (BR): hadynyah/E+/GettyImages; p. 26: Thomas_EyeDesign/Vetta/GettyImages; p. 30: Education Images/Universal Images Group/GettyImages; p. 32 (George): snapphoto/E+/GettyImages; p. 32 (airport): Philippe TURPIN/Photononstop/Photolibrary/GettyImages; p. 32 (Diane): Vesnaandjic/E+/GettyImages; p. 32 (car): lisegagne/E+/GettyImages; p. 34: Whiteway/E+/GettyImages; p. 35 (wrench): TokenPhoto/E+/GettyImages; p. 35 (TR): John E. Kelly/Photodisc/GettyImages; p. 36: pixelfusion3d/iStock/Getty Images Plus/GettyImages; p. 37 (drain): belovodchenko/iStock/Getty Images Plus/GettyImages; p. 37 (plane): incposterco/E+/GettyImages; p. 37 (smoke): Harrison Shull/Aurora/GettyImages; p. 37 (land): Sierralara/RooM/GettyImages; p. 38 (forest): Ro-Ma Stock Photography/Photolibrary/GettyImages; p. 39: Howard Shooter/Dorling Kindersley/GettyImages; p. 40: VCG/Contributor/Visual China Group/GettyImages; p. 41: Travel Ink/Gallo Images/The Image Bank/GettyImages; p. 42: SolStock/iStock/Getty Images Plus/GettyImages; p. 43: Doug Armand/Oxford Scientific/GettyImages; p. 44: Wilfried Krecichwost/DigitalVision/GettyImages; p. 45: cglade/E+/GettyImages; p. 46 (TL): Lew Robertson/StockFood Creative/GettyImages; p. 46 (TC): Alina555/iStock/Getty Images Plus/GettyImages; p. 46 (TR): Jose Luis Pelaez Inc/Blend Images/GettyImages; p. 47 (photo 1): Hemera Technologies/PhotoObjects.net/Getty Images Plus/GettyImages; p. 47 (photo 2): Picturenet/Blend Images/Photodisc/GettyImages; p. 47 (photo 3): Zoran Milich/Photodisc/GettyImages; p.47 (photo 4): DragonImages/iStock/Getty Images Plus/GettyImages; p. 48 (TR): BrianAJackson/iStock/Getty Images Plus/GettyImages; p. 48 (CR): reka prod./Westend61/GettyImages; p. 49 (TR): simazoran/iStock/Getty Images Plus/Getty Image; p. 49 (CR): ONOKY - Eric Audras/Brand X Pictures/GettyImages; p. 49 (BR): michaeljung/iStock/Getty Images Plus/GettyImages; p. 50: leaf/iStock/Getty Images Plus/GettyImages; p. 52 (TL): IP Galanternik D.U./E+/GettyImages; p. 52 (TR): Lady-Photo/iStock/Getty Images Plus/GettyImages; p. 54: Westend61/GettyImages; p. 55 (CR): Andy Sheppard/Redferns/GettyImages; p. 55 (BR): by Roberto Peradotto/Moment/GettyImages; p. 56 (L): Mint/Hindustan Times/GettyImages; p. 56 (R): Michael Runkel/imageBROKER/GettyImages; p. 57: Bettmann/GettyImages; p. 58 (TL): Bettmann/GettyImages; p. 58 (BR): Ron Levine/Photographer's Choice/GettyImages; p. 59: Windsor & Wiehahn/Stone/GettyImages; p. 60: Javier Pierini/Stone/GettyImages; p. 61: blackred/iStock/Getty Images Plus/GettyImages; p. 62: izusek/iStock/Getty Images Plus/GettyImages; p. 63: ADRIAN DENNIS/AFP/GettyImages; p. 67: Greg Vaughn/Perspectives/GettyImages; p. 68: Caiaimage/Robert Daly/GettyImages; p. 69 (TL): marco wong/Moment/GettyImages; p. 69 (TR): Oscar Wong/Moment Open/GettyImages; p. 69 (CL): Otto Stadler/Photographer's Choice/GettyImages; p. 69 (CR): David Hannah/Lonely Planet Images/GettyImages; p. 69 (BL): LOOK Photography/UpperCut Images/GettyImages; p. 69 (BR): lightkey/E+/GettyImages; p. 70: Thomas Kokta/Photographer's Choice RF/GettyImages; p. 71 (Calgary Farmers' Market): Ken Woo/Calgary Farmers' Market; p. 71 (WWF): © naturepl.com/Andy Rouse/WWF; p. 72: Christian Hoehn/Taxi/GettyImages; p. 73 (TL): Rosanna U/Image Source/GettyImages; p. 73 (TC): Mark Weiss/Photodisc/GettyImages; p. 73 (TR): i love images/Cultura/GettyImages; p. 73 (BL): monkeybusinessimages/iStock/Getty Images Plus/GettyImages; p. 73 (BC): Photo and Co/The Image Bank/GettyImages; p. 73 (BR): Alija/E+/GettyImages; p. 74 (stonehenge): Maxine Bolton/EyeEm/GettyImages; p. 74 (people): Peter Dennis/GettyImages; p. 74 (boats): De Agostini/M. Seemuller/De Agostini Picture Library/GettyImages; p. 75 (bigfoot): Big_Ryan/DigitalVision Vectors/GettyImages; p. 75 (footprints): Danita Delimont/Gallo Images/GettyImages; p. 76: Steve Bronstein/Stone/GettyImages; p. 77: kbeis/DigitalVision Vectors/GettyImages; p. 78: mediaphotos/Vetta/GettyImages; p. 79 (T): Oscar Garces/CON/LatinContent Editorial/GettyImages; p. 81: Theo Wargo/Getty Images North America/GettyImages; p. 82 (TL): ColorBlind Images/Blend Images/GettyImages; p. 82 (TR): track5/E+/GettyImages; p. 83: imagenavi/GettyImages; p. 84 (TL): John Wildgoose/Caiaimage/GettyImages; p. 84 (TR): Bloomberg/GettyImages; p. 84 (CL): Chris Ryan/Caiaimage/GettyImages; p. 84 (CR): numbeos/E+/GettyImages; p. 84 (BL): Tom Merton/OJO Images/GettyImages; p. 84 (BR): Ariel Skelley/Blend Images/GettyImages; p. 85 (TL): marcoventuriniautieri/E+/GettyImages; p. 85 (TR): Anadolu Agency/GettyImages; p. 85 (CL): Caspar Benson/GettyImages; p. 85 (CR): Jake Olson Studios Blair Nebraska/Moment/GettyImages; p. 86 (house): Peter Baker/GettyImages; p. 86 (traffic): Levi Bianco/Moment/GettyImages; p. 86 (bike): Billy Hustace/The Image Bank/GettyImages; p. 86 (using mobile): SolStock/E+/GettyImages; p. 87: Image Source/DigitalVision/GettyImages; p. 89: Caiaimage/Paul Bradbury/Riser/GettyImages; p. 90: Dawid Garwol/EyeEm/GettyImages; p. 92: FatCamera/E+/GettyImages; p. 93: c.Zeitgeist/Everett/REX/Shutterstock; p. 94 (TR): shapecharge/E+/GettyImages; p. 94 (BR): borgogniels/iStock/Getty Images Plus/GettyImages; p. 95: Lucidio Studio, Inc./Moment/GettyImages.

1 That's my kind of friend!

1 Complete these descriptions with the words from the list.

1. Eric is so ___modest___! He always has such great ideas and never takes any credit for them.

2. The Wongs like meeting new people and having friends over for dinner. They're one of the most _____ couples I know.

3. You can't trust Alice. She always promises to do something, but then she never does it. She's pretty _____.

4. James wants to be an actor. It's hard to break into the business, but his family is very _____ of his dream.

5. I never know how to act around Lisa! One minute she's in a good mood, and the next minute she's in a bad mood. She's so _____.

- ☑ modest
- ☐ outgoing
- ☐ supportive
- ☐ temperamental
- ☐ unreliable

2 Opposites

A Complete the chart by forming the opposites of the adjectives in the list. Use *in-* and *un-*. Then check your answers in a dictionary.

- ☑ attractive
- ☐ reasonable
- ☐ helpful
- ☐ flexible
- ☐ dependent
- ☑ competent
- ☐ reliable
- ☐ popular
- ☐ formal
- ☐ experienced
- ☐ cooperative
- ☐ sensitive

Opposites with *in-*		Opposites with *un-*	
incompetent	_____	unattractive	_____
_____	_____	_____	_____
_____	_____	_____	_____

incompetent

B Write four more sentences using any of the words in part A.

1. <u>Alan is very incompetent at work. He makes a lot of mistakes.</u>

2. _____

3. _____

4. _____

5. _____

3 Add *who* or *that* to the conversation where necessary.
Put an *X* where *who* or *that* is not necessary.

A: I'm looking for someone _____ *X* _____ I can go on vacation with.

B: Hmm. So what kind of person are you looking for?

A: I want to travel with someone _____ is easygoing and independent.

B: Right. And you'd probably also like a person _____ is reliable.

A: Yeah, and I want someone _____ I know well.

B: So why don't you ask me?

A: You? I know you too well!

B: Ha! Does that mean you think I'm someone _____ is high-strung, dependent, and unreliable?

A: No! I'm just kidding. You're definitely someone _____ I could go on vacation with.
So, . . . what are you doing in June?

4 Complete the sentences with *who* or *that* and your own information or ideas.

1. I generally like to go out with people <u>who are easygoing and have a sense of humor</u> .

2. I'd rather travel with someone _____ .

3. I don't really want a roommate _____ .

4. My classmates and I like teachers _____ .

5. My best friend and I want to meet people _____ .

6. Most workers would prefer a boss _____ .

7. Some people don't like stingy types _____ .

8. I don't want to have inflexible friends _____ .

9. I feel comfortable discussing my problems with friends _____ .

10. My favorite friends are people _____ .

5 Two of a kind?

A Read the article. What six personality types are discussed?

DO OPPOSITES ATTRACT EACH OTHER?

Some psychologists believe that we are attracted to people who seem to have the characteristics that we wish we had. For example, if you love music but don't play an instrument, you might be attracted to someone who is a musician. Being with that person allows you to be close to something that is important to you and that you want more of in your life.

Because people are very complex, we can be attracted to several different kinds of people who are our opposites in one way or another. So let's take a look at six principal kinds of characteristics in people, and you can decide which type you are most like and which type is your opposite.

Let's begin with introverted and extroverted people. Introverted people often spend a lot of time inside their minds and can be quiet and reserved. Extroverted people enjoy getting out and spending time with other people. If opposites attract, then there will always be an interest between introverted and extroverted people. Introverted people will get out of their minds and into the world with their extroverted friends or partners, while extroverted people will appreciate the quiet space of the inner world of their introverted friends or partners.

Then there are people who relate to the world from a thinking perspective and others who relate to it from a feeling perspective. Thinkers can be cool and objective in their judgments, while feelers may be warm and passionate about theirs. Because people who spend a lot of time thinking want to feel deeply too, they may be attracted to a feeling kind of person. And someone who is very aware of their own powerful feelings may enjoy the company of a relaxed and logical thinker.

Two other characteristics are those of people who use their five senses to understand the world we live in as opposed to those who use their intuition. Sensing people are very aware of the present moment; they are realistic and practical people. Intuitive people, on the other hand, often spend their time in a future of infinite possibilities where their imagination is as free as a bird. The attraction here could be that intuitive people realize they need the practical know-how of sensing people in order to make their dreams come true. Likewise, the sensors are attracted to the imaginative possibilities they see in intuitive people.

These three different pairs of personality characteristics – the introvert and the extrovert, the thinker and the feeler, and the sensor and the intuitive – are of course found in each individual person. Yet many psychologists believe that a person will more often use one characteristic of each pair, in the same way that people use either their left hand or their right. And, according to the idea that opposites attract, the left hand needs the right hand in the same way that the right hand needs the left!

B Based on the information in the article, what kind of people are you attracted to? Circle the words. Then, using the idea that opposites attract, complete the next sentence with the type of person *you* must be.

1. I am more attracted to a person who is (introverted / extroverted). Therefore, I am _____.

2. I am more attracted to a person who is a (thinker / feeler). Therefore, I am a _____.

3. I am more attracted to a person who is the (sensing type / intuitive type). Therefore, I am a _____.

C Do you agree with the kind of person you seem to be according to part B? Why or why not?

6 Match the clauses in column A with the most suitable clauses in column B.

A	B
1. I like it _____	**a.** when someone criticizes me in front of other people.
2. I don't mind it _____	**b.** when people are easygoing and friendly.
3. It upsets me _____	**c.** when rich people are stingy.
4. It embarrasses me _____	**d.** when people are a few minutes late for an appointment.

7 Write sentences about these situations. Use the expressions in the box.

I love it . . .	I can't stand it . . .	I don't like it . . .
It upsets me . . .	It bothers me . . .	I don't mind it . . .
I really like it . . .	It makes me happy . . .	It makes me angry . . .

1. _I don't like it when_
people cut in line.

2. _____

3. _____

4. _____

5. _____

6. _____

8 **What are some things you like and don't like about people? Write two sentences about each of the following. Use the ideas in the pictures and your own ideas.**

1. What I really like:

<u>I love it when someone</u>

<u>is generous and gives me flowers.</u>

<u>It makes me happy when</u>

_____

2. What I don't like:

<u>It bothers me when</u>

_____

_____

3. What doesn't bother me:

<u>I don't mind it when</u>

_____

_____

_____

4. What upsets me:

<u>It upsets me when</u>

_____

_____

_____

9 It really bugs me!

Choose one thing from Exercise 8 that really embarrasses, bothers, or upsets you. Write two paragraphs about it. In the first paragraph, describe the situation. In the second paragraph, say why this situation is difficult for you and describe a situation you would prefer.

> It really embarrasses me when someone is too generous to me. Recently, I dated a guy who was always giving me things. For my birthday, he bought me an expensive necklace, and he treated me to dinner and a movie.
>
> The problem is, I don't have enough money to treat him in the same way. I'd prefer to date someone I have more in common with. In fact, my ideal boyfriend is someone who is sensible and saves his money!

_____

_____

_____

_____

_____

_____

_____

_____

10 Choose the correct word to complete each sentence.

1. I can tell Simon anything, and I know he won't tell anyone else. I can really _____ him. (believe / treat / trust)

2. Kay has a very high opinion of herself. I don't like people who are so _____. (egotistical / temperamental / supportive)

3. It bothers me when people are too serious. I prefer people who are _____ and have a good sense of humor. (easygoing / inflexible / reliable)

4. I like it when someone expresses strong _____. Hearing other people's views can really make you think. (accomplishments / compliments / opinions)

5. Lisa is very rich, but she only spends her money on herself. She's very _____. (generous / modest / stingy)

2 Working 9 to 5

1 What's your job?

A Match the jobs with their definitions.

A/An . . .	is a person who . . . .
1. comedian __f__	**a.** researches environmentally friendly technologies
2. green researcher _____	**b.** helps students with their problems
3. guidance counselor _____	**c.** controls a company's brand online
4. organic food farmer _____	**d.** creates computer applications
5. social media manager _____	**e.** grows food without chemicals
6. software developer _____	**f.** makes people laugh for a living

B Write a definition for each of these jobs: accountant, fashion designer, and flight attendant.

1. _An accountant is someone who_ _____

2. _____

3. _____

2 Challenging or frightening?

A Which words have a positive meaning, and which ones have a negative meaning? Write *P* or *N*.

awful __N__   fantastic _____

boring _____   fascinating _____

challenging _____   frightening _____

dangerous _____   interesting _____

difficult _____   rewarding _____

B Write about four more jobs you know. Use the words in part A and gerund phrases.

1. _I think being a comedian would be fascinating._ _____

2. _____

3. _____

4. _____

5. _____

3 Career choices

A Match each career and the most appropriate job responsibility.

Careers		Job responsibilities
work	for an airline	do research
	with computers	teach discipline and fitness
	as a high school coach	learn new software programs
be	a university professor	work independently
	a writer	travel to different countries

B Use the information from part A and gerund phrases to complete this conversation.

Teri: So, what kind of career would you like, Jack?

Jack: Well, I'm not exactly sure. _____Being a writer_____ could be interesting. Maybe blogging about something I'm interested in.

Teri: Hmm. I don't know if I'd like that because I'd have to write every day.

Jack: What do you want to do, then?

Teri: Well, I'm not sure either! I'd love _____. I'd really enjoy being with teenagers all day and _____. On the other hand, I'd be interested in _____.

Jack: Really? What would you like about that?

Teri: Well, I'd love _____ all over the world.

Jack: Oh, I could never do that! I think it would be very tiring work.

C Write a short conversation like the one in part B. Use the remaining information in part A or your own ideas.

A: So, what kind of career would you like?

B: Well, I'm not exactly sure. _____

A: That sounds interesting. But I wouldn't like it because _____

B: What do you want to do then?

A: Well, I'd love _____

B: _____

A: _____

4 What a job!

A Read the magazine interviews. Write the correct job title above each interview. There are two extra jobs.

☐ architect   ☐ freelance artist   ☐ preschool teacher   ☐ university professor
☐ bus driver   ☐ house painter   ☐ train conductor   ☐ website designer

TELL US ABOUT YOUR JOB

1 _____

I have always enjoyed making things, and what's more interesting than building something that people will use for years? The challenge of discovering exactly how a space needs to be constructed for maximum usefulness and beauty is what makes me wake up with a smile. I often work late at the office, but that's part of the job.

2 _____

Working for yourself is hard because you're responsible for everything. If no one calls you and asks you to work for them, you have to go out and look for work. Luckily, I now have some regular clients. I paint pictures for some expensive hotels. Right now, I'm doing some paintings for the rooms of a new hotel in Hawaii.

3 _____

My friends say my work is less demanding than theirs, but I work just as hard as they do. I spend a lot of time alone because my job can't begin until all the construction work is completed. Usually, the rooms look great when I've finished my work. Sometimes I don't like the colors that customers choose, but I have to do what they want.

4 _____

These days a lot of people are doing what I've been doing for fifteen years. I work closely with my clients to find out exactly what they want to show on the Internet and how to make it look as attractive as possible. My work requires a good eye for art, a command of clear and precise language, and of course, knowledge of the latest technology.

5 _____

I meet all kinds of people: some are the best and others aren't so good. Sometimes I have a great conversation with someone I've never met before. And of course, I have my regulars, people I see every day, and we talk about life. But I always keep my attention on the road.

6 _____

Being with kids all day isn't for everyone, but I love it. I take care of children when their parents are away. I do all kinds of things – I teach, I play games, and I read books. I make sure the children are safe and happy. I have a lot of responsibility, but I love my job. It's very rewarding work even though the pay isn't great.

B Underline the words and phrases that helped you find the answers in part A.

5 First, use words from the list to complete each job title. Then choose the best expressions to compare the jobs in each sentence.

☐ assistant   ☐ decorator   ☐ painter   ☐ walker
☐ counselor   ☐ instructor   ☐ ranger   ✓ worker

1. A child-care _____worker_____ doesn't earn _____as much as_____ an accountant.
   ✓ as much as   ☐ greater than   ☐ worse than

2. A chef's _____ has _____ a waiter.
   ☐ worse hours than   ☐ not as good hours   ☐ as worse hours as

3. A dog _____ is _____ a student intern.
   ☐ more interesting than   ☐ not as boring as   ☐ better paid than

4. A house _____ earns _____ a camp counselor.
   ☐ as bad as   ☐ more than   ☐ not more than

5. A park _____ is _____ a landscaper.
   ☐ as bad as   ☐ not as well paid as   ☐ worse than

6. Being a yoga _____ is _____ being a professor.
   ☐ more than   ☐ as much as   ☐ not as difficult as

7. Being an interior _____ is _____ being a sales assistant.
   ☐ greater than   ☐ earns more than   ☐ more interesting than

8. A guidance _____ has _____ a gardener.
   ☐ more responsibility than   ☐ not more than   ☐ not as long as

6 Complete these sentences with the correct prepositions. Some of the prepositions may be used more than once. More than one answer may be possible.

☐ as
☐ at
☐ in
☐ on
☐ with

1. Chonglin works _____ the best Chinese restaurant in Los Angeles.

2. I think working _____ other people is more fun than working alone.

3. I would hate working _____ the media. It would be nerve-racking!

4. Working _____ a dance instructor sounds great.

5. Working _____ an office is less interesting than working _____ a cruise ship.

7 **Use the words in parentheses to compare the jobs.**

> **Assistant** needed at an outdoor swimming pool. Must be able to swim. Responsible for keeping pool and changing rooms clean. $12/hour. Tues.–Fri. 12–7.

> **Learn web design!**
> In search of a bright young person to work as an intern for an advertising agency. Some clerical work. $15/hour. Mon.–Fri. 9–5.

1. A: An assistant at a swimming pool has shorter hours than an intern.
   (shorter hours)

   B: Yes, but working as an intern is more interesting than being a swimming pool assistant.
   (interesting)

> **Travel agency** needs energetic people. Knowledge of a second language is a plus. Mostly answering the phone. $18/hour. Flexible hours. Five vacation days a year.

> **Tutors** in math, science, English, and music wanted at private summer school. Challenging work with gifted teenagers. Salary negotiable. Mon.–Sat. 3–7.

2. A: Working in a
   (better benefits)

   B: Yes, but working
   (challenging)

> **Tennis instructor** needed at summer camp for 12- and 13-year-olds. Must be excellent tennis player and good with kids. $18/hour. Mon.–Fri. 1–7.

> Tour company seeks **guide** to lead bus tours. Great attitude and good speaking voice a must! Fun work, but must be willing to work long hours. $15/hour.

3. A: _____
   (make as much money)

   B: _____
   (work longer hours)

> City seeks **taxi drivers** for morning shift. No experience necessary; driver's license required. $15/hour plus tips. Mon.–Thu. 7 A.M.–2 P.M.

> **Office assistant** required in small, friendly office. Computer skills an advantage. Interesting work. Some management skills necessary. $20/hour. 6-day week.

4. A: _____
   (a shorter work week)

   B: _____
   (less boring)

8 Choose four pairs of jobs from the box below to compare.
Say which job you would prefer and give two reasons.

- a graphic designer/a TV news director
- an architect/a teacher
- a guidance counselor/a coach
- a doctor/a musician
- a police officer/a politician
- a secret agent/a psychiatrist
- working on a construction site/working in an office
- being self-employed/working for a company

Example: _Working as a TV news director sounds more interesting than being a graphic designer._
A TV news director has more responsibility than a graphic designer.
Also, directing the news is better paid.

1. _____

2. _____

3. _____

4. _____

3 Lend a hand.

1 Would you mind . . . ?

A Complete the request for each situation.

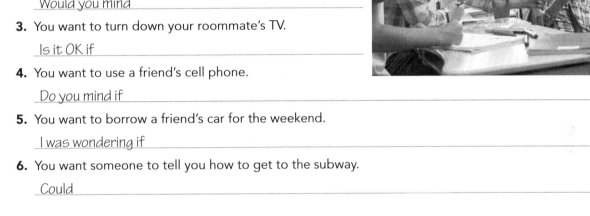

1. You want to borrow a classmate's pen.

Can I borrow your pen?

2. You want a classmate to give you a ride home after class.

Would you mind

3. You want to turn down your roommate's TV.

_Is it OK if_

4. You want to use a friend's cell phone.

Do you mind if

5. You want to borrow a friend's car for the weekend.

I was wondering if

6. You want someone to tell you how to get to the subway.

Could

B Think of four more things you would need to have done if you were going on a long vacation. Write requests asking a friend to do the things.

1. _Could you water the plants?_

2. _____

3. _____

4. _____

5. _____

2 **Accept or decline these requests. For requests you decline, give excuses. Use the expressions in the chart or expressions of your own.**

Accepting	Declining
That's OK, I guess.	Sorry, but . . .
I'd be glad to.	I'd like to, but . . .
Fine. No problem.	Unfortunately, . . .

1. **A:** Can I use your computer? My computer crashed.

   B: *Sorry, but I'm going to use it myself in a few minutes.*

2. **A:** I've just finished this ten-page paper. Could you check it for me, please?

   B: _____

3. **A:** I was wondering if I could stay at your place for a week while my landlord fixes the roof.

   B: _____

4. **A:** Would you mind if I used your cell phone to make a long-distance call to Nigeria?

   B: _____

3 **Look at the pictures and write the conversations. Speaker A makes a request. Speaker B declines it. Each speaker should give a reason.**

1. **A:** *Could you carry these boxes for me? I have a bad back.*

   B: *Sorry, but I have a bad back, too.*

2. **A:** _____

   B: _____

3. **A:** _____

   B: _____

4 Getting what you want

A Scan the magazine article about making requests. What strategies can you use for less formal requests? What strategies can you use for more formal requests?

The Art of Making Requests

When you make a request, it helps to be clear about two things: Firstly, how well do you know the other person? Secondly, how important is it for you to get what you want? Are you willing to take "no" for an answer?

Let's say that you would like to borrow someone's car to go out on Friday night. Because borrowing a car is a big favor, we can assume that you'd probably only ask someone you know well for this favor. In general, when making requests of friends or close acquaintances, you can use a less formal approach.

Now let's imagine that it's very important for you to have that car on Friday night; you have to have it. In that case, you can let the other person know in a less formal, direct way. Here are two possible strategies:

1. Make a statement with *need*: "I need to borrow your car."
2. Use an imperative: "Please lend me your car."

By avoiding questions, this approach makes it more difficult for the other person to say no. If you are willing to put the other person in a possibly awkward situation, then this is definitely the clearest, and perhaps most effective, way of getting what you want.

But maybe you expect the other person to say no, and you can live with that. This attitude allows you to have a cooler, more objective perspective, so you can make your request in a more formal, indirect way.

Here are some examples:

3. Ask about ability: "Could/Can you lend me your car?"
4. Be polite – use *may*: "May I borrow your car?"
5. Ask for permission: "Would it be OK if I borrowed your car?"
6. Express curiosity: "I wonder if I could borrow your car."
7. State the request negatively: "I don't suppose you could lend me your car."
8. Apologize: "I hope you don't mind my asking, but could I borrow your car?"
9. Give a hint: "I have plans for Friday night, but I don't have a car."

This approach gives the other person a polite way to refuse if, for any reason, they don't want to or cannot lend you their car. And even though you know the person well, taking a more formal approach proves to the listener that you realize what a big favor you're asking. It shows them respect and appreciation – which makes it more likely that you'll get the result you want!

B Read the article. Check (✓) if each request is less formal or more formal. Then write the correct number from the article (1–9) for each type of request. Only eight of the numbers will be used.

	Less formal	More formal	Type
1. Close the door.	☐	☐	___
2. It's really cold in here.	☐	☐	___
3. Could you possibly move your car?	☐	☐	___
4. May I borrow your dictionary?	☐	☐	___
5. I was wondering if you could help me with this assignment.	☐	☐	___
6. I need some help moving to my new apartment.	☐	☐	___
7. I'm sorry, but I can't stand loud music.	☐	☐	___
8. I don't suppose I could borrow your camera.	☐	☐	___

5 Nouns and verbs

A Complete this chart. Then check your answers in a dictionary.

Noun	Verb	Noun	Verb
apology	*apologize*	invitation	
compliment		permission	
explanation		request	

B Check (✓) the phrase that describes what each person is doing.

1. Don't worry. I know you didn't mean to break it.
   - ☐ returning a favor
   - ☐ accepting an apology

2. I really like your new haircut.
   - ☐ giving a reason
   - ☐ giving a compliment

3. Can I borrow your laptop?
   - ☐ asking for a favor
   - ☐ giving a gift

4. I can't lend you my bike because I need it myself.
   - ☐ declining a request
   - ☐ accepting an invitation

5. Could you help me cook dinner?
   - ☐ making a request
   - ☐ returning a compliment

6 Choose the correct words.

1. My phone didn't work for a week. The phone company _____ an apology and took $20 off my bill. (accepted / denied / offered)

2. A friend of mine really loves to _____ compliments, but he never gives anyone else one. I don't understand why he's like that. (do / owe / receive)

3. Diane is always talking on the phone. She makes a lot of calls, but she rarely _____ mine. Maybe she never listens to her voice mail! (makes / offers / returns)

4. I need to _____ a favor. Could you please give me a ride to school tomorrow? My bike has a flat tire! (ask for / give / turn down)

7 Use these messages to complete the phone conversations. Use indirect requests.

```
———— Message ————
For: Silvia

Ms. Karen Landers called.
Her flight arrives at 7 P.M. on
Tuesday. Please meet her in the
International Arrivals area.
```

```
———— Message ————
For: Mike

Mr. Maxwell called yesterday.
The meeting is on Thursday at
10:30 A.M. Don't forget to bring
your report.
```

```
———— Message ————
For: Mark

Ed called this morning. Can he
borrow your scanner? If he can,
when can he pick it up?
```

```
———— Message ————
For: Katy

Andy Chow called earlier. Are you
going to the conference tomorrow?
What time does it start?
```

1. A: Is Silvia Vega there, please?

   B: No, she isn't. Would you like to leave a message?

   A: Yes, please. This is Karen Landers calling from Toronto.

   Could you tell her *that my flight arrives at 7 P.M. on Tuesday* _____ ?

   Would _____ ?

   B: OK, I'll give her the message.

2. A: Can I speak to Mark, please?

   B: I'm afraid he's not here. Do you want to leave a message?

   A: Yes, please. This is Ed. Please _____ .

   And if it's OK, could you _____ ?

   B: Sure, I'll leave him the message.

3. A: Could I speak to Mike, please?

   B: I'm sorry, but he's not here right now.

   A: Oh, OK. This is Mr. Maxwell. I'd like to leave a message.

   Could _____ ?

   Could _____ ?

4. A: I'd like to speak to Katy, please.

   B: She's not here right now. Can I take a message?

   A: Yeah. This is Andy Chow.

   Can _____ ?

   And would _____ ?

   B: OK, I'll give Katy your message.

8 Complete the conversation with the information in the box. Add any words necessary and use the correct form of the verbs given.

- ☐ ask Kelly to get some soda
- ☐ borrow some money
- ☑ borrow your wireless speaker
- ☐ bring a big salad
- ☐ buy dessert
- ☐ don't be late

Dan: So, is there anything I can do to help for the party?

Mark: Yeah. I have a list here. Would it be all right
if I borrowed your wireless speaker ?
Mine isn't working very well.

Dan: Sure. And I'll bring two extra speakers. We'll have amazing sound.

Mark: Thanks.

Dan: No problem. Now, what about food?

Mark: Well, I thought maybe a salad. Would you mind _____, too?

Dan: Well, OK. And how about drinks?

Mark: Well, could you _____? And please tell her _____. Last time we had a party, she didn't arrive till eleven o'clock, and everyone got really thirsty!

Dan: I remember.

Mark: One more thing – I was wondering if you could _____.

Dan: Um, sure. All right. But, uh, would you mind if I _____ to pay for it?

---

9 Rewrite these sentences. Find another way to say each sentence using the words given.

1. Can I use your cell phone?
   Would it be OK if I used your cell phone? (OK)

2. Please ask Annie to stop by and talk to me.
   _____ (would)

3. Could I borrow your guitar?
   _____ (wonder)

4. Would you ask Mitch what time he's coming over?
   _____ (could / when)

5. Lend me your hairbrush.
   _____ (mind)

4 What happened?

1 Complete these news stories using the verbs from the box.

1.

- ☐ broke
- ☐ drank
- ☐ found
- ☐ heard
- ☐ locking
- ☐ shouted
- ☐ stayed
- ☐ waiting
- ☑ went
- ☐ wondered

WOMAN TRAPPED IN BATHROOM FOR 20 DAYS

A 69-year-old grandmother in Paris _____went_____ to the bathroom – and _____ there for twenty days. What happened? As she was _____ the door, the lock _____. She could not open the door. She _____ for help, but no one _____ her because her bathroom had no windows. After nearly three weeks, the woman's neighbors _____ where she was. Firefighters broke into her apartment and _____ her in a "very weakened" state. While she was _____ to be rescued, she _____ warm water.

2.

- ☐ became
- ☐ behaving
- ☐ checking in
- ☐ decided
- ☐ entered
- ☐ had
- ☐ opened
- ☐ showed
- ☐ sleeping

TIGER CUB FOUND IN LUGGAGE

A woman was _____ strangely when she _____ the Bangkok airport. While she was _____ for an overseas flight, she _____ difficulty with a very large bag. The check-in clerk _____ suspicious and _____ to X-ray the bag. The X-ray _____ an image that looked like an animal. When airport staff _____ the bag, they saw that a baby tiger was _____ under lots of toy tigers. The tiger was taken to a rescue center for wildlife, and the woman was arrested.

2 **Join each sentence in column A with an appropriate sentence in column B. Use *as, when,* or *while* to join the sentences.**

A	B
I was crossing the road.	My racket broke.
I was using my computer.	A car nearly hit me.
We were playing tennis.	The water got cold.
I was taking a shower.	I burned my finger.
I was cooking dinner.	It suddenly stopped working.

1. As I was crossing the road, a car nearly hit me.

2. _____

3. _____

4. _____

5. _____

3 **Complete these conversations. Use the simple past or the past continuous of the verbs given.**

1. **A:** Guess what happened to me last night!
   As I ___was getting___ (get) into bed, I
   _____ (hear) a loud noise like
   a gunshot in the street. Then the phone
   _____ (ring).

   B: Who was it?

   A: It was Luisa. She always calls me late at
   night, but this time she had a reason.
   She _____ (drive) right past
   my apartment when she _____
   (get) a flat tire. It was very late, so while
   we _____ (change) the tire,
   I _____ (invite) her to spend
   the night.

2. **A:** I'm sorry I'm so late, Erin. I was at the
   dentist.

   B: Don't tell me! While you _____
   (sit) in the waiting room, you
   _____ (meet) someone
   interesting. I know how you are, Matt!

   A: Well, you're wrong this time. The dentist
   _____ (clean) my teeth when she
   suddenly _____ (get) called away
   for an emergency. So I just sat there waiting
   for two hours with my mouth hanging open!

4 Lost and found

A Read this news story. Who is it about? Where did it take place?

Thank you, Andre Botha!

On December 6, 2015, Andre Botha was in the water, watching the big waves at the Pipeline off the island of Oahu, Hawaii, when he noticed something strange. The two-time world bodyboarding champion realized that professional champion surfer Evan Geiselman was in big trouble. Since the Pipeline has some of the biggest waves in the world and is considered to be the most dangerous place on the planet for surfing, situations like this are, unfortunately, not uncommon.

Botha realized that the surfer, who had entered the inside of a huge wave and was riding it, was knocked off his surfboard when the wave crashed on him. Normally a surfer will come up to the surface of the water a few moments after falling off the board. But there was no sign of Geiselman. Botha began to swim on his bodyboard as fast as he could to where the surfboard was being thrown around by the huge waves. When he reached the

Surfing at the Pipeline

surfboard, he saw Geiselman, who looked like he might be dead. The surfer was unconscious and his face was turning blue as Botha tried to bring him back to life in the water. Botha breathed into Geiselman's mouth and hit him on the chest to get him breathing again. Then he began to swim to shore with the surfer's unconscious body. Two lifeguards swam out to meet him, and they brought Geiselman to a hospital.

Surfers and bodyboarders agree that Evan Geiselman would probably not be alive today if Andre Botha had not rescued him. They don't always agree about which sport is best, but surfers and bodyboarders do agree that taking care of each other in the big waves is important. This respect and care for people is a wonderful part of these exciting sports.

Bodyboarding

B Use the article to answer these questions.

1. In what sport is Andre Botha a two-time champion?

_____

2. What sport does Evan Geiselman excel at as a champion?

_____

3. Where is the Pipeline located?

_____

4. What is one way you can help an unconscious person start breathing?

_____

5. Who brought Geiselman to the hospital?

_____

6. What helps make bodyboarding and surfing such wonderful sports?

_____

5 Think of a real or imaginary problem like the one in Exercise 4. Write two paragraphs. In the first paragraph, describe your problem. In the second, say how you solved it.

_____
_____
_____
_____
_____
_____
_____
_____
_____

> A couple of years ago, I got lost in the mountains. I was hiking when it suddenly got foggy. I was really frightened because I couldn't see anything, and it was getting cold. I decided to put up my tent and stay there for the night.
>
> While I was putting up my tent, though, the fog began to clear. . . .

6 Choose the correct verbs to complete the story.

Grammar note: After

In sentences using *after* that show one past event occurring before another, the clause with *after* usually uses the past perfect.

After she **had called** her friend, her cell phone battery died.

Andy and I ___had just gotten___ engaged, so we
(just got / had just gotten)

went to a jewelry store to buy a wedding ring. We _____ a ring when a
(just chose / had just chosen)

masked man _____. After the robber _____ Andy's
(came in / had come in)   (took / had taken)

wallet, he _____ the ring. I _____ it to him when the
(demanded / had demanded)   (just handed / had just handed)

alarm _____ to go off, and the robber _____. We were
(started / had started)   (ran off / had run off)

so relieved! But then the sales assistant _____ us we had to pay for the ring
(told / had told)

because I _____ it to the robber. We _____ her
(gave / had given)   (just told / had just told)

that we wouldn't pay for it when the police _____ and
(arrived / had arrived)

_____ us! What a terrible experience!
(arrested / had arrested)

7 What a story!

A Choose the best headline for each of these news stories.

What a disaster! **What a triumph!**

What an emergency! **What a lucky break!** **What a dilemma!**

1. _____
Karen Lane was seven months pregnant when she and her husband, Scott, went on vacation to a small **remote** island off the coast of South America. On the first night, Karen was in a lot of pain. There were no doctors on the island, so Scott called a hospital on the **mainland**. They told him they could not send a helicopter because a typhoon was coming. During the night, Karen thought she was going to die. Luckily, the typhoon had passed over the island by the following morning. A helicopter picked Karen up and took her to the hospital – just in time for her to have a beautiful baby girl.

2. _____
Serena Mills was very sick for several months before her final exams this summer. She couldn't study at all. Her parents suggested she should **skip** a year and take the exams the next summer. **Remarkably**, Serena suddenly got well just before the exams, spent two weeks studying, and got the highest grade in her class!

3. _____
Mark Blaine had waited years for a **promotion**. Finally, a week ago, he was offered the position he had always wanted – Regional Manager. On the same day, however, he won $6 million in the lottery. Mark's wife wants him to **resign** from his job and take her on a trip around the world. Mark says he cannot decide what to do.

B Look at the words in bold in the articles. What do you think they mean?

remote _____   skip _____   promotion _____

mainland _____   remarkably _____   resign _____

8 Complete the sentences. Use the simple past, the past continuous, or the past perfect of the verbs given.

1. In 2011, two divers _____*discovered*_____ (discover) the remains of a 200-year-old shipwreck while they _____ (dive) off the coast of Rhode Island, in the eastern United States.

2. After an art show _____ (open) in New York, it was discovered that someone _____ (hang) a famous painting by Henri Matisse upside down.

3. In 2015, workers _____ (find) a chemistry lab from the 1840s while they _____ (repair) a building at the University of Virginia in the United States. The lab was behind a wall of the current building.

4. Chile's Calbuco volcano _____ (surprise) residents of Santiago when it erupted in 2015. Before that, an eruption of Calbuco _____ (not happen) for over 40 years.

9 **Read this situation. Then use the information and clues to complete the chart. Write the name of each reporter and each country. (You will leave one square in the chart blank.)**

Ms. Johnson

Ms. Marshall

Mr. James

Mr. Grant

Mr. Simpson

Five news reporters – two women and three men – arrived for an international conference on Sunday, Monday, and Tuesday.

No more than two people came on the same day. The reporters came from five different countries.

Clues

The women: Ms. Johnson and Ms. Marshall

The men: Mr. James, Mr. Grant, and Mr. Simpson

The countries: Australia, Mexico, Brazil, Singapore, and the United States

The arrivals:

• Mr. Simpson arrived late at night. No one else had arrived that day.

• Ms. Johnson and Mr. Grant arrived on the same day.

• The man who came from Singapore had arrived the day before.

• The reporters who came from Brazil and Australia arrived on the same day.

• Mr. James and the woman who came from Brazil arrived on Tuesday, after Mr. Grant.

• The reporter from Australia arrived the day after the person who came from the United States.

• Mr. Grant came from North America but not the United States.

Reporters' countries and arrival days		
Sunday	Name: _____	Name: _____
	Country: _____	Country: _____
Monday	Name: _____	Name: _____
	Country: _____	Country: _____
Tuesday	Name: _____	Name: _____
	Country: _____	Country: _____

5 Expanding your horizons

1 Complete these sentences. Use words from the box.

- ☐ confident
- ☐ curious
- ☐ depressed
- ☑ embarrassed
- ☐ fascinated
- ☐ uncertain
- ☐ uncomfortable
- ☐ worried

1. In my country, people never leave tips. So when I first went abroad, I kept forgetting to tip servers. I felt really __embarrassed__ .

2. The first time I traveled abroad, I felt really _____. I was alone, I didn't speak the language, and I didn't make any friends.

3. I just spent a year in France learning to speak French. It was a satisfying experience, and I was _____ by the culture.

4. At first I really didn't like shopping in the open-air markets. I felt _____ because so many people were trying to sell me something at the same time.

5. When I arrived in Lisbon, I was nervous because I couldn't speak any Portuguese. As I began to learn the language, though, I became more _____ about living there.

6. Before I went to Alaska last winter, I was very _____ about the cold. But it wasn't a problem because most buildings there are well heated.

7. When I was traveling in Southeast Asia, I couldn't believe how many different kinds of fruit there were. I was _____ to try all of them, so I ate a lot of fruit!

8. It was our first trip to Latin America, so we were _____ about what to expect. We loved it and hope to return again soon.

2 Imagine you are going to travel to a country you have never visited before. Write sentences using the factors and feelings given. Then add another sentence explaining your feelings.

Factors	Feelings
public transportation	anxious (about)
shopping	comfortable (with)
the climate	curious (about)
the food	enthusiastic (about)
the language	fascinated (by)
the money	nervous (about)
the music	uncertain (about)
the people my age	uncomfortable (with)

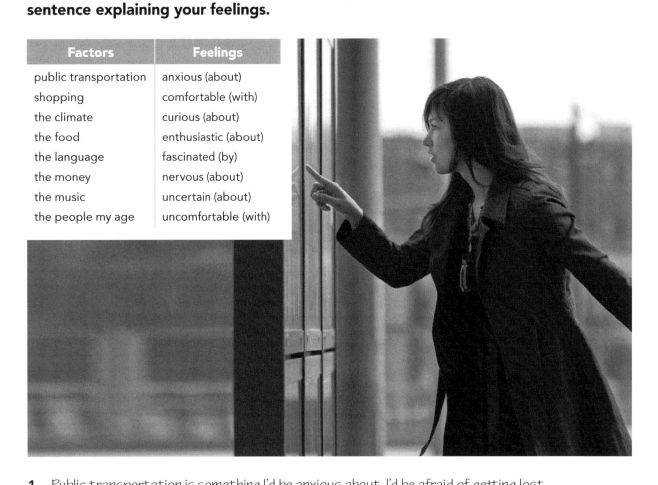

1. _Public transportation is something I'd be anxious about. I'd be afraid of getting lost._

2. _____

3. _____

4. _____

5. _____

6. _____

7. _____

8. _____

9. _____

3 Culture shock!

A Make a list of four pieces of advice to help people feel comfortable about traveling abroad.

B Scan the article about cultural differences. Where can you find articles like this? Who was it written for?

Culture Shock

Each society has its own beliefs, attitudes, customs, behaviors, and social habits. These things give people a sense of who they are and how they are supposed to behave.

People become conscious of such rules when they meet people from different cultures. For example, the rules about when to eat vary from culture to culture. Many North Americans and Europeans organize their timetables around three mealtimes a day. In other countries, however, it's not the custom to have strict rules like this – people eat when they want to, and every family has its own timetable.

When people visit or live in a country for the first time, they are often surprised at the differences between this culture and the culture in their own country. For some people, traveling abroad is the thing they enjoy most in life; for others, cultural differences make them feel uncomfortable, frightened, and insecure. This is known as "culture shock."

When you're visiting a foreign country, it is important to understand and appreciate cultural differences. This can help you avoid misunderstandings, develop friendships more easily, and feel more comfortable when traveling or living abroad.

Here are several things to do in order to avoid culture shock.

1 Instead of criticizing, enjoy the new customs you discover each day on your trip as much as possible.

2 If you read or understand the language, read a local newspaper or listen to the radio to find out what news they're likely to be talking about.

3 Talk to people in order to understand their ideas about their own country as well as their thoughts about yours.

4 Remember the proverb, "When in Rome, do as the Romans do." It's a great way to start learning new things!

5 For instance, try one new thing every day, like a food you've never had before, instead of choosing something on the menu that you can have in your own country.

6 Read a book about the history of the place you are in so you will understand it better while you are there.

7 Go to concerts, museums, theatrical performances, and sporting events to appreciate the culture of this country.

8 Remember that traveling is an educational experience, so be ready to question the stereotypes you may have of another country, and learn about the stereotypes people in that country may have about the place you come from.

C Read the article. Use your own words to write definitions for these words.

1. culture _____

2. culture shock _____

3. appreciate _____

4. stereotypes _____

D After reading the article, would you make any changes to the pieces of advice you listed in part A?

4 Complete these sentences by giving information about customs in a country you know.

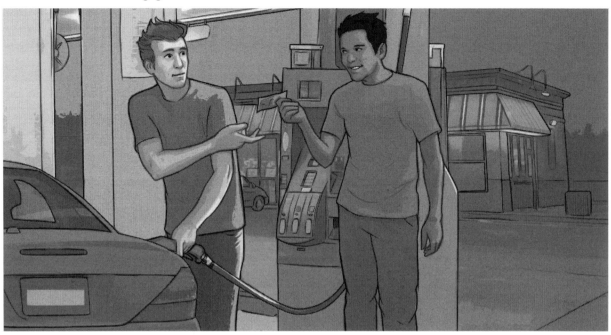

1. If you go for a long ride in a friend's car, *it's the custom to offer to pay for some of the expenses.*

2. When a friend graduates from school or college, _____

_____

3. If you borrow something from a friend, _____

_____

4. When a friend invites you to dinner, _____

_____

5 Contrasting customs

A Read the information about the different customs and find four pairs of countries with contrasting customs. Write the countries on the lines below.

Country	Custom
Brazil	Friends kiss each other three or four times on the cheeks as a greeting.
Denmark	People generally arrive on time for most occasions.
Egypt	People allow their hosts to treat them to meals in restaurants.
France	Service is usually included in the price of a meal in restaurants.
Japan	People bow when they see or meet someone they know.
New Zealand	People usually pay for their own meals in restaurants.
Spain	People usually arrive late for most appointments.
United States	People leave a tip of 15–20 percent in restaurants.

1. *Brazil and Japan* _____   3. _____

2. _____   4. _____

B Read these five cross-cultural situations. Write sentences describing what the visitors did wrong. Use the expressions in the box.

you're (not) supposed to

you're (not) expected to

it's (not) the custom to

it's (not) acceptable to

1. Enni is from Denmark. When she was on vacation in Spain, some Spanish friends invited her to dinner at 9:00. She arrived at exactly 9:00, but her friends had not even arrived home yet.

   In Spain, you're expected to

2. Kayla is from the United States. During her first week in Paris, she went to a restaurant with some new friends. She was so happy with the service that she left a tip of 20 percent. Her friends were a little embarrassed.

   In France,

3. James is from New Zealand. When he went to Egypt, he was invited to dinner at a restaurant. When the bill came, he offered to pay for his dinner. His Egyptian friend was kind of upset.

   In Egypt,

4. Clara is from Brazil. She was working for a year in Osaka, Japan. One day, when she saw a Japanese co-worker in a bookstore, she went to say hello and kissed him on the cheeks. Her friend was very surprised.

5. Brian is from Canada. He was on vacation in Bali, Indonesia, and some new friends invited him to a temple to watch a special dance performance. He arrived on time wearing a clean T-shirt and shorts, but they said he couldn't go inside the temple because he wasn't dressed properly.

6 Complete these sentences with information about yourself (1–4) and about a country you know well (5–8).

1. One reason I'd feel homesick abroad is _____

2. Something that would fascinate me would be _____

3. Traveling alone is something _____

4. Getting used to hot weather is one thing _____

5. In _____, it's the custom to _____

6. If you have good service in a restaurant, _____

7. You're expected to _____ when _____

8. It's just not acceptable to _____ if _____

7 Write about living in a foreign country. In the first paragraph, write about two things you would enjoy. In the second paragraph, write about two things you might worry about.

If I lived in Colombia, I'd enjoy learning about the music scene – the local bands and singers who are popular there. Another thing I'd be fascinated by is . . . However, one thing that I'd be nervous about is the food. It might be very different from what I know. Something else I might be uncomfortable with is . . .

That needs fixing.

1 What's wrong with it?

A What can be wrong with these things? Put these words in the correct categories.
(Most words go in more than one category.)

| bike | blouse | car | carpet | chair | glasses | plate | sink | tablecloth |

chipped	cracked	dented	leaking	scratched	stained	torn

B What is wrong with these things? Use the words in part A to write a sentence about each one.

1. _The car is scratched._ OR **2.** _____ **3.** _____

There's a scratch on the car. _____

4. _____ **5.** _____ **6.** _____

_____ _____ _____

7. _____ **8.** _____ **9.** _____

_____ _____ _____

2 Problems, problems, problems!

A Scan the articles in *Consumer* magazine. Who would read articles like these? Why?

George's Class Trip

George Humphrey is a Spanish teacher at Crockett College in Duluth, Minnesota. Last year, George took his summer class from Duluth to Madrid, Spain. At the end of the six-week trip, George and the twenty students had a delayed flight at the airport in Madrid when they were coming home. Because of the six-hour delay in Madrid, they missed their plane from New York to Minnesota. Everyone had to stay at a hotel in New York City, and they all spent a lot more money than they had expected. They were also more than 24 hours late when they finally got back to Duluth. When George asked the airline office in New York to pay for their hotel and restaurant bills, the airline refused.

George contacted *Consumer* magazine. We talked to a representative of the airline office in Madrid and discovered that, in Europe, airlines must pay for delays – but that does not apply to airlines in the U.S. However, because the delay first occurred in Madrid, George and each student received 400 euros. George was very pleased, especially for his students. In his email to us, George wrote that he believes the law regarding airline delays needs changing in the U.S.

Diane's Vacation

Diane Gleason is a clothing designer in Cincinnati, Ohio. For her vacation last year, she decided to go somewhere she had never been – the southwestern part of the U.S. When she arrived at the airport in Phoenix, Arizona, she rented a beautiful red convertible for her trip. She planned to drive from Phoenix to the Grand Canyon to go hiking with friends for a few days. After she left the airport, Diane spent the night in Phoenix. The next morning, Diane discovered that someone had stolen the car from the parking lot. She called the car-rental agency, and they told her she was responsible for the cost of the car because she had left the keys in it. They would not let her rent another car until she paid for the stolen one. Diane didn't know what to do. She went back to the motel and contacted *Consumer* magazine.

We called the rental agency, and they told us that Diane had not bought special insurance for a stolen car. We told the agency that Diane needed help: she was all alone and feeling worried and depressed about what happened. The agency suggested that we contact Diane's credit card company. We did, and they told us that Diane was protected because of her credit card. They would pay for the stolen car! By evening, Diane had rented another car from the same agency and, that night, she had dinner at the Grand Canyon with her friends.

B Read the articles and complete the chart. Did George and Diane receive money?

	Problems	What *Consumer* magazine did	Received money?	
			Yes	No
1. George's trip	*delay in Madrid*		☐	☐
2. Diane's vacation			☐	☐

3 Choose appropriate verbs to complete the sentences. Use passive infinitives (*to be* + past participle) or gerunds.

> **Language note: Verbs ending in -*en* or -*n***
>
> Some verbs are formed by adding -*en* or -*n* to a noun or adjective.
> These verbs mean "to make more of something."
>
> | Noun | Verb | Adjective | Verb |
> |------|------|-----------|------|
> | length | → length**en** | loose | → loose**n** |
> | (make something longer) | | (make something looser) | |

 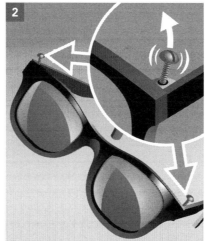 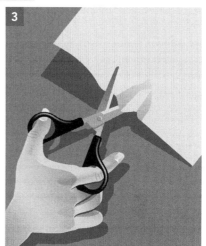

☑ lengthen ☐ loosen ☐ sharpen ☐ shorten ☐ tighten ☐ widen

1. This jacket is too short.

   It needs to be lengthened.   OR

   It needs lengthening.

2. The screws on these glasses are too loose.

   They need _____

3. The blades on these scissors are too dull.

   They need _____

4. This faucet is too tight.

   It needs _____

5. These pants are too long.

   They need _____

6. This street is too narrow.

   It needs _____

4 **Complete the conversation. Use *keep*, *keeps*,
need, or *needs* with passive infinitives or
gerunds of the verbs given.**

Jack: Guess what? Someone broke into my car last night!

Mia: Oh, no. What did they take?

Jack: Nothing! But they did a lot of damage. The lock
needs to be repaired (repair). And
the window _____
(replace).

Mia: It was probably some young kids having "fun."

Jack: Yeah, some fun. I think they had a party in my car! The seats
_____ (clean).

Mia: How annoying. Does the car drive OK?

Jack: No, it feels strange. The gears _____
(stick), so they _____ (fix). And the brakes
_____ (check) right away.

Mia: Well, I guess you're lucky they didn't steal it!

Jack: Yeah, lucky me.

5 **Write about something you bought that had something wrong with it.
In the first paragraph, describe the problem. In the second paragraph,
explain what you did about it.**

Recently, I bought an espresso machine. While I was unpacking it, I could see it was already damaged. The glass carafe was chipped and needed to be replaced. And to make matters worse, the machine leaked!
I took it back to the store. I was worried because the machine had been on sale, and I had lost my receipt. Luckily, the clerk didn't ask me for it. She said a lot of customers had recently had the same problem, and she gave me a better machine at the same price.

_____
_____
_____
_____
_____
_____
_____
_____

Paul will fix it!

A Match each problem with the repair needed.

PAUL'S REPAIR SHOP

ITEM	PROBLEM	REPAIR NEEDED
1. dishwasher	doesn't work ___f___	a. tighten and glue the legs
2. DVD player	DVD is stuck _____	b. repair the wire
3. speakers	wire is damaged _____	c. remove the DVD
4. dresser	mirror is cracked _____	d. repaint the door
5. stove	metal door is scratched _____	e. replace the mirror
6. table	legs are loose _____	f. check the motor

B Write a sentence describing each problem. Then add a sentence describing the action needed to fix it. Use passive infinitives or gerunds.

1. _The dishwasher doesn't work. The motor needs to be checked._ OR
The motor needs checking.

2. _____

_____

3. _____

_____

4. _____

_____

5. _____

_____

6. _____

_____

C Think of three items you own that are damaged (or were damaged) in some way.
Write a sentence describing each problem. Then write another sentence
describing the action needed to fix it.

1. _____

_____

2. _____

_____

3. _____

_____

7 Complete the sentences with the correct forms of the words in the box.

☐ chip	✓ drop	☐ freeze	☐ scratch
☐ clean	☐ fix	☐ jam	☐ stick
☐ die	☐ flicker	☐ leak	☐ torn

1. This cell phone is driving me crazy! My calls keep ___*dropping*___.

2. Your computer screen is so dirty. It needs to be _____.

3. Something is wrong with your TV screen. It keeps _____. It's time to get a new one.

4. I hate this printer. It keeps _____. The copies won't come out.

5. Be careful – your cup is _____. I don't want you to cut yourself.

6. The buttons on this remote control keep _____. Do you have something to clean it with?

7. Do you realize your jeans are _____ in the back?

8. Your bathroom faucet keeps _____. Do you want me to try to fix it?

9. My new glasses already have a _____ on one of the lenses. How did that happen?

10. Did your laptop _____ again? I find that so annoying.

11. This old scanner doesn't work at all anymore. It needs to be _____.

12. The battery in my cell phone keeps _____. I should buy a new one.

7 What can we do?

1 Use the information in the pamphlet and the verbs and prepositions given below to change the sentences from the active to the passive.

HERE ARE JUST SOME OF THE DANGERS FACING YOU AND YOUR CHILDREN.

The water we drink

1. Agricultural runoff is contaminating the water supply.
2. Chlorine and other additives have ruined the taste of our drinking water.

The food we eat

3. Certain agricultural pesticides have caused new illnesses.
4. Pollution from cars and trucks is destroying our crops.

The air we breathe

5. Factories are releasing dangerous chemicals.
6. Breathing smog every day has damaged many people's health.

The world we live in

7. The lack of rainfall has created more severe droughts.
8. Global warming is threatening our forests and wildlife.

Join Save Our Planet today!

1. _The water supply is being contaminated due to agricultural runoff._ (due to)

2. _____ (by)

3. _____ (by)

4. _____ (because of)

5. _____ (by)

6. _____ (as a result of)

7. _____ (through)

8. _____ (by)

2 Verbs and nouns

A Complete the chart.

Verb	Noun	Verb	Noun
contaminate	contamination	educate	_____
contribute	_____	_____	pollution
_____	creation	populate	_____
deplete	_____	protect	_____
_____	destruction	_____	reduction

B Write four sentences like the ones in Exercise 1 using words from the chart.

Example: _Many rivers and streams have been badly contaminated by industrial waste._

1. _____

2. _____

3. _____

4. _____

3 Choose the correct words or phrases.

1. Green organizations are trying to save rain forests that have been _threatened_ by developers and farmers. (created / ruined / threatened)

2. One way to inform the public about factories that pollute the environment is through _____ programs on TV. (agricultural / educational / industrial)

3. In many countries around the world, threatened animal and plant species are being _____ by strict laws. (created / polluted / protected)

4. Agricultural pesticides are _____ the soil in many countries. (damaging / eating up / lowering)

5. _____ is an enormous problem in many large cities where whole families can only afford to live in one room. (pollution / poverty / waste)

El Yunque rain forest

4 How safe is the fleece you are wearing?

A Scan the title and first two paragraphs of this article. What is fleece?
Do you own clothing made of fleece? What clothing?

The Fleece that Came to Dinner

Today, half of the clothing bought by people is made of a synthetic fiber. And that figure is almost 70% in the developing world. Synthetics – or fibers that are created by science, not by nature – are very attractive to customers because, for example, some of them are water-resistant, which is particularly desirable for rain gear and hiking shoes. Moreover, synthetics don't require the amount of water, labor, and land that is needed to cultivate cotton and other natural fibers.

One of the most popular synthetic fabrics is called fleece, a name that originally referred to the wool from a sheep, which is still used to make fall and winter clothes. But in the twenty-first century, the word "fleece" refers to the inexpensive, lightweight, and often water-resistant synthetic material that more and more people are wearing today.

One of the most interesting things about fleece is the fact that it can be made from recycled plastic bottles. This means that fleece can be far less expensive than wool or other natural fibers. For many people, recycling plastic bottles is thought of as friendly to the natural environment since we are reusing the plastic, not burying it in the ground or dumping it in the oceans. However, in the last few years, scientists have discovered that fleece may not be as environmentally friendly as we once supposed.

Scientists are now finding very small particles of plastic at the bottom of the ocean that they believe are the remains of fleece that is washed in washing machines every day all over the world. When it is washed, more than 1,500 particles may separate from a fleece product into the water. When that water is drained, some of it will make its way back into the lakes, rivers, and oceans of our world. That is what seems to be happening now. When the synthetic particles reach natural bodies of water, the plastic is going to be eaten by fish because it looks like food to them. And sooner or later, those fish are going to be caught, delivered to the food market, and end up on your plate at dinner.

What can be done? Shall we return to more costly, heavier, and traditional natural fibers such as cotton and wool? Are people willing to spend more money to possibly save the environment? Or is economics so important to people who have very little money that they believe they cannot afford to give up their synthetic fibers?

B Read the article. Check (✓) the true statements. For statements that are false, write the true information.

1. ☐ In the developing world, 50% of people buy clothing made of synthetic fiber.

2. ☐ The word "fleece" originally meant sheep's wool.

3. ☐ Fleece is made from recycled plastic bottles.

4. ☐ More than 2,000 particles of fleece may separate during washing.

5. ☐ Fortunately, fish will not consume particles of fleece.

6. ☐ We now know that people are going to stop using fleece because of its dangers.

5 World issues

A Match the nouns and definitions.

Nouns		Definitions
1. infectious diseases	_d_	**a.** physical actions that are meant to cause destruction or injury
2. global warming	___	**b.** a period of time when businesses are not doing well and a large number of people cannot find jobs
3. government corruption	___	**c.** an extreme lack of money
4. famine	___	**d.** illnesses that can be passed on to other people
5. political unrest	___	**e.** a situation in which people do not have enough food
6. poverty	___	**f.** a situation in which citizens become angry or violent due to their dissatisfaction with their government
7. recession	___	**g.** illegal or dishonest activity by people with political power
8. violence	___	**h.** a situation in which a number of people are not working because they cannot find jobs
9. unemployment	___	**i.** an increase in the world's average temperatures

B Choose the correct noun from part A to complete each sentence. You will not use all of the words.

1. It seems like there are more dangerous _____ these days, like swine flu and the Zika virus.

2. During the recent _____, 30 percent of the businesses in my town closed, and a large part of the population didn't have jobs.

3. There's so much _____ in this city. I'm afraid to walk on the streets alone at night because I don't feel safe.

4. Before you travel to a foreign country, make sure there are no dangerous political situations going on there. It can be unsafe to visit countries that are experiencing

_____.

5. In the 1800s, a large portion of Irish potato crops were destroyed by disease. Because potatoes were a major part of the Irish diet, there was a major _____ and over 1.5 million people died.

6. People in this country don't trust the police or city officials because there is a lot of _____.

6 Complete the conversations. Use the expressions in the box and the information in the list.

| One thing to do . . . | The best way to fight . . . |
| Another thing to do . . . | One way to help . . . |

- ☑ complain to the Parks Department about it
- ☐ create more government-funded jobs
- ☐ create more public housing projects
- ☐ organize a public meeting to protest the threat of public property
- ☐ educate young people about its dangers
- ☐ report it to the local newspaper
- ☐ donate money to charities that provide shelters and food

A new housing development?

1. **A:** A big housing developer wants to build an apartment complex in Forest Hill Park. I think that's terrible, but what can we do?

   B: _One thing to do is to complain to the Parks Department about it._

   A: That's a good idea.

   B: _____

2. **A:** Personally, I'm worried about violence in the city. The streets are not safe at night.

   B: _____

3. **A:** You know, there's a lot of corruption in our city government.

   B: _____

   A: Yeah, the bad publicity might help to clean things up a bit.

4. **A:** There are so many unemployed people in this city. I just don't know what can be done about it.

   B: _____

5. **A:** What worries me most is the number of homeless people on the streets.

   B: _____

   A: I agree.

   B: _____

7 **Complete the sentences using the present continuous passive or the present perfect passive. Then suggest a solution to each problem.**

1. A lot of jobs _____*have been lost*_____ (lose) in recent years.
   One way to deal with unemployment _____*is to bring more businesses*_____ into the area.

2. These days, a lot of endangered animals _____ (kill) by hunters and poachers.
   The best way to stop this practice _____

   _____.

3. During the past few years, lots of trees _____ (destroy) by acid rain.
   One thing to do about it _____

   _____.

4. Underground water _____ (contaminate) by agricultural pesticides.
   The best way to deal with the problem _____

   _____.

5. Too many people _____ (affect) by infectious diseases in the past few years.
   The best way to stop this _____

   _____.

8 **Write two paragraphs about a charity, an organization that helps people. In the first paragraph, describe what the charity does. In the second paragraph, explain why you think the charity is useful.**

A good charity in my city is Shelter. This organization works to reduce the number of homeless people on our streets. Shelter believes the best way to do this is to . . .

Shelter is my favorite charity because homelessness is, in my opinion, the greatest problem facing my city. Many people cannot find jobs, and . . .

8 Never stop learning.

1 Choose the correct words or phrases.

1. I'm interested in human behavior, so I'm planning to take a class in _____.
(geography / psychology / math)

2. I want to take a course in _____, such as commerce or accounting.
(education / business / social science)

3. I'd prefer not to study _____ because I'm not very comfortable in hospitals. (engineering / new media / nursing)

4. I'd really like to work in Information Technology, so I'm thinking of taking courses in _____.
(computer science / finance / English)

2 What would you prefer?

A Write questions with *would rather* or *would prefer* using the cues.

1. take a science class / an art class

   Would you rather take a science class or an art class? OR
   Would you prefer to take a science class or an art class?

2. study part time / full time

   _____

3. have a boring job that pays well / an exciting job that pays less

   _____

4. take a long vacation once a year / several short vacations each year

   _____

B Write answers to the questions in part A.

1. _____
2. _____
3. _____
4. _____

3 Love it or leave it

A First, complete speaker A's questions with four things you would not like to do. Use ideas in the box or your own ideas.

> learn to play the accordion
> learn clothing design
> learn how to repair watches
> study sociology
> take a class in personal finance
> take a cooking class

1. **A:** _Do you want to learn to play the accordion?_

   B: _I'd rather not. I'd prefer to learn to play the piano._   OR

   I'd prefer not to. I'd rather learn to play the piano.

2. **A:** Do you want to _____?

   B: _____

3. **A:** Would you like to _____?

   B: _____

4. **A:** Do you want to _____?

   B: _____

5. **A:** Would you like to _____?

   B: _____

B Now write responses for speaker B. Use the short answers *I'd rather not* or *I'd prefer not to* and say what you would prefer to do.

4 Answer these questions and give reasons.

1. On your day off, would you rather stay home or go out?

   I'd rather stay home than go out because _____

2. Would you prefer to have a cat or a bird?

   _____

3. Would you rather live in the city or the country?

   _____

4. When you entertain friends, would you rather invite them over for dinner
   or take them out to a restaurant?

   _____

5. Would you prefer to see a new movie at the theater or download it and watch it at home?

   _____

5 Online learning, the schools of the future?

A Have you taken an online class? Would you like to? Would you prefer to study online rather than at school? Write your answers.

_____

_____

B Read the online newspaper article. Underline the sentences that contain the answers to these questions.

1. What is a MOOC?

2. Why do so few students complete a MOOC?

3. Do professors who teach MOOCs think that they are as difficult as courses taken in a classroom?

4. What are critics of MOOCs afraid of?

FREE COLLEGE FOR EVERYONE?

posted 21st of August

A revolution in education is going to happen. **Massive Online Open Courses (MOOCs for short) are designed for students who cannot afford, cannot get to, or simply don't want to attend classes in a university classroom.** MOOCs are going to be of great importance to economically disadvantaged people, as well as people who live far from a university campus. The only requirement to attend a MOOC is access to a computer with an Internet connection, which is becoming more common each day.

Many MOOCs are created by top professors in their fields who teach at prestigious universities in the U.S., like Princeton, Harvard, and Stanford. These professors may teach online courses at their universities, but with a MOOC they can reach students all over the world. At the moment, not all universities accept academic credit for a MOOC. However, almost half of the professors who have taught a MOOC believe that the coursework is as demanding as the work done in a traditional university class. Many of these professors are not paid for teaching MOOCs by their universities; they do it because they want to

make education available to everyone, they love teaching, and they enjoy being able to communicate with so many students online.

MOOC students do not pay tuition, which is perhaps the greatest appeal of these courses. Most professors do not even require students to buy textbooks, which can be very expensive as well. This further reduces the cost of education. On the other hand, despite the affordability of MOOCs, MOOC students do not receive diplomas, which may lessen their appeal. Students may receive certification if they

pass the course, but of the 33,000 students enrolled in MOOCs today, **the completion rate is strikingly low, at only 10%. Because a MOOC doesn't cost anything, students don't have to worry about losing money if they decide to drop the class. And many of them ultimately do.**

So while there are upsides to MOOCs, they are not without their critics. **Some professors fear that in the future there may be two kinds of university courses: expensive and superior courses at a traditional university where small groups of students meet in classes with their professors, and inexpensive and inferior massive online courses where students will never meet their professors nor even their fellow students.** These critics also point out that students must be disciplined self-starters to be successful in a MOOC and that students often develop the skills of perseverance, time-management, and self-discipline by learning together with other students in a traditional university classroom.

C Write answers to these questions.

1. Do you think MOOCs are going to be the courses of the future? Why or why not?

_____

_____

2. What do you see as the main advantage of MOOCs? The main disadvantage?

_____

_____

D What would you prefer to take as a MOOC: a humanities course (such as literature, art, or history) or a science course (such as biology, chemistry, or engineering)? Why did you choose that course?

6 Complete the sentences with *by* + gerund. Use *not* if needed. Use the ideas in the box or your own information.

cook at home	eat out	go out more often	study dance
eat good food	exercise regularly	stay home	use social media

cook at home

study dance

use social media

1. A good way to enjoy the weekend is _not by staying home but by going out with friends._
2. A good way to keep in touch with old friends is _____
3. You can make new friends _____
4. The best way to save money is _____
5. You could stay in shape _____
6. I stay healthy _____
7. One way to learn self-confidence is _____

7 Choose the correct words or phrases.

1. Robin shows her _____ by volunteering to help people with cancer. (competitiveness / communication skills / concern for others)

2. When I was young, I didn't understand the importance of _____. But when I started paying my own bills, I realized it's an important skill. (money management / cooperation / perseverance)

3. I learned _____ from my parents. They taught me the importance of using my imagination and making art. (creativity / courtesy / self-confidence)

4. Gina always gets upset with people who disagree with her. I wish she would show more _____. (perseverance / self-confidence / tolerance)

5. I recently joined a choir, and I love it. But you need a lot of _____, because you have to practice the same piece of music for weeks before you're ready to perform it! (cooperation / perseverance / time management)

8 Personal qualities

A Read about each student in these descriptions and choose a suitable quality for each one.

- ☐ competitiveness
- ☐ cooperation
- ☐ creativity
- ☐ perseverance
- ☐ self-confidence
- ☐ self-discipline
- ☐ time management
- ☐ tolerance

1. Alex is always on time for everything. He's never even five minutes late. He keeps track of everything on his calendar. I wish I were as good at _____ as Alex is.

2. Frank finds school very hard, but no one tries harder than he does. He always spends the whole weekend at the library trying to keep up with his studies. He shows great

   _____ .

3. Melissa always wants to do better than everyone else. In school, she always tries to get the best grades. Her favorite sport is field hockey because she's the best player in the school. No one needs to teach Melissa _____ .

4. Jennifer has more _____ than any of her classmates. She writes fascinating stories that show she has a wonderful imagination. She's also very artistic and does very interesting paintings.

B Write two similar descriptions of people you know. Either use two of the qualities you didn't use in part A or choose other qualities.

1. _____

   _____

   _____

   _____

2. _____

   _____

   _____

   _____

9 My way

A List two methods of learning each of these skills.

1. become a good guitarist

<u>*by teaching myself*</u>

<u>*by taking lessons*</u>

2. improve my writing ability in English

3. become a more confident public speaker

4. learn more about personal finance

5. become skilled at auto repair

6. learn a new computer program

my first guitar

15 years later

B Which of the two methods in part A would you prefer to use to develop each skill? Write sentences using *would rather (not)* or *would prefer (not)*. Give reasons.

1. <u>*I'd rather learn guitar by teaching myself than by taking lessons.*</u>

<u>*I'd prefer not to take lessons because they're expensive.*</u>

2.

3.

4.

5.

6.